SOME OTHER GARDEN

BOOKS BY JANE URQUHART

FICTION

The Whirlpool

Storm Glass (short stories)

Changing Heaven

Away

The Underpainter

POETRY

*I Am Walking in the Garden of His Imaginary Palace:
Eleven Poems for Le Notre*

False Shuffles

The Little Flowers of Madame de Montespan

Some Other Garden

SOME OTHER GARDEN

JANE URQUHART

PHOTOGRAPHS BY JENNIFER DICKSON

Copyright © 2000 by Jane Urquhart

Eleven Poems for Le Notre first published in 1982 as *I Am Walking in the Garden of His Imaginary Palace* by Aya Press. Copyright © 1982 by Jane Urquhart

The Little Flowers of Madame de Montespan first published in 1983 by The Porcupine's Quill, Inc. Copyright © 1983, 1995 by Jane Urquhart.

All rights reserved. The use of any part of this publication reproduced, transmitted in any form or by any means, electronic, mechanical, photocopying, recording, or otherwise, or stored in a retrieval system, without the prior written consent of the publisher – or, in case of photocopying or other reprographic copying, a licence from the Canadian Copyright Licensing Agency – is an infringement of the copyright law.

CANADIAN CATALOGUING IN PUBLICATION DATA

Urquhart, Jane, 1949–
Some other garden

Poems.
Originally published in 2 volumes under titles: The little flowers of Madame de Montespan and I am walking in the garden of his imaginary palace
ISBN 0-7710-8669-5

1. Montespan, Françoise-Athénaïs de Rochechouart de Mortemart, marquise de, 1641-1707 – Poetry.   2. Louis XIV, King of France, 1638-1715 – Poetry.   3. Le Nôtre, André, 1613-1700 – Poetry.   4. Gardens – France – Versailles – Poetry.   I. Title.   II. Title: Little flowers of Madame de Montespan.   III. Title: I am walking in the garden of his imaginary palace.

PS8591.R68S65 2000   C811'.54   C00-931546-2
PR9199.3.U7S65 2000

We acknowledge the financial support of the Government of Canada through the Book Publishing Industry Development Program for our publishing activities. We further acknowledge the support of the Canada Council for the Arts and the Ontario Arts Council for our publishing program.

Some of these poems may have undergone minor revisions.

Jacket and interior photos by Jennifer Dickson, R.A.

Typeset in Aldus by M&S, Toronto
Printed and bound in Canada

McClelland & Stewart Ltd.
The Canadian Publishers
481 University Ave.
Toronto, Ontario
M5G 2E9
www.mcclelland.com

1   2   3   4   5   04   03   02   01   00

For Guy Ducornet and Rikki Ducornet

And for Anne Pippin Burnett and Virgil Burnett

CONTENTS

I.
*THE LITTLE FLOWERS OF
MADAME DE MONTESPAN*

THE BAROQUE BED

Shadow / 5
Museum / 7
The Baroque Bed / 8
The One Before / 9
The Grotesque Geometry / 11
Bright Rumours / 12
Venetian Gondoliers at Versailles / 13
Your Hand Carves / 14
An Amusement in Twelve Movements / 15

ARTIFICIAL FIRE

Games and the King / 19
Words / 20
All Around the Palace / 21
The King Advises His Son / 22
Choosing the Subject of the Fountain / 24
Notes for the Machine at Marly / 26
I Am Speaking the Difficult / 28
The Palace Closed / 29
Anonymous Journal / 31
Planet / 33

Terre Sauvage or The King's Nightmare / 35
Necessary Pause / 37
Birds / 38
Marly le Roi / 40
Turning Back at Dusk / 42

THE POISONED SHIRT

Some Other Garden / 45
The Porcelain Trianon / 46
The Anonymous Journal / 48
Evidence / 49
Le Roi S'Amuse / 50
The Vermilion Box / 52
Horses / 54
The Years Departing / 56
The Poisoned Shirt / 57

GLASS COFFINS

Anonymous Journal / 61
Winter of 1709 / 63
Silenced / 65
Lady Reason / 66
One Memory of Opening / 68
Doctor Fagon / 69
Glass Coffins / 71
Hall of Mirrors / 72

II.
ELEVEN POEMS FOR LE NOTRE / 73

Photo Credits / 88

I.

THE LITTLE FLOWERS
OF MADAME DE MONTESPAN

La Vallière, so 'tis said,
Is losing favour fast
The King goes to her bed
With boredom unsurpassed

Now Montespan takes o'er
Things, as we've seen before,
From hand to hand get passed

– Eighteenth-century street song

The Baroque Bed

SHADOW

The sun decides to
enter from the garden

moving on the carpet
he touches all your furniture
crawls under your closet door
investigates your wardrobe

moves his arm across
your memories
substituting light
and heat and silence

he erases last year's
conversations with the stars
changes the contents of your mirrors
invents an alternative
palette for your crystal

scrapes his nails across brocade
revealing tangled threads
like contours on a map

he polishes your tables
his brilliance clings to cutlery
till spoons become large
bright incisions
all across the grain

a weight of gold and heat
he stops   burning
at the flesh of your neck

you are the only shadow in the room

MUSEUM

The objects he had touched shifted. Walls crumbled. Courtiers vanished with crystal, cutlery, diamonds in their back pockets. Frescoes peeled. The garden grew.

Absolute dispersal. The vast auction lasted for years. There was vandalism, forgery. And then the relocation, loose fragments drawn into new configurations.

Catalogued items: a nail from the shoe of a horse. A broken mirror from a private chamber. A scrap of paper mapping out the garden. A cutting of brocade.

Saved artifacts: seven prayers he breathed in haste. Four denials. A goblet full of memories. An urn for everything forgotten.

There, the display case exhibiting his women: passion, wit and reason. Sorrow, poison, order. Jewellery, costume and a broken quill pen.

Objects of pleasure: the prow of an imported golden gondola, the torn sail . . . a toy Spanish galleon. Fireworks, a miniature pageant, false porcelain from the first Trianon. Twelve masks, playing cards, dancing slippers. A stuffed swan.

The palace: gold leaf particles . . . a fractured fresco. This piece of marble, once part of a fountain. And then this candelabra, found not too long ago, intact.

THE BAROQUE BED

From the framed centre
a cloth folds
its golden threads
brush the floor

brocade lambs graze
unicorns prance
a shepherdess in the shorn
world loses
her slipper in the chaos

white peacock
feathers at the edge
knots and tassels
dance in the air

they call this passion

I am lost in the fabric
smothered by your private furniture

I know the loom that dreamed this bed

THE ONE BEFORE

The one before
walked in these rooms
gazed in these mirrors
and searched her thighs for flaws

opening his cupboard
pouring this decanter
her mind set sail for landscapes
where you might stop
to choose a gift for her

a snowdrop pressed inside a book
birds frozen in a cage

the hours filled with
preservation of her flesh
her hair and face and muscle
till laying down her brush
she felt your absence speak

as though you hadn't nodded when
you passed her in the garden
or kept a place
beside you at the table

now I fill these rooms
and search the mirrors
I listen to the sound of strings
caressed by fountains

those imperfections in the glass
her face   thighs
lost in silver

the ghost travels with me
to your chamber

THE GROTESQUE GEOMETRY

My dress conceals
the structure of the rooms

shaping afternoons into
a grotesque geometry

everything I touch
billows over edges

these sheets
           those plumes
the satin skirt I fling aside

I appear in windows
I dissolve in doorways

outside my skin
your pulse is moving

growing through the silence
into confusion

BRIGHT RUMOURS

At night the window glass
reveals the self
the lamps cause fire

in the facets of my jewellery
and at my throat
bright rumours whisper

outside the garden turns away
and the windowpanes
reveal ourselves

outside
there is a gulf of darkness
where everything is watching

the other worlds have
vanished

in the morning
we're unable to see

VENETIAN GONDOLIERS AT VERSAILLES

Their Republic opened out towards the sea. Long fingers extended to the lagoon. They returned by different routes in a city like a maze.

Here they sail over a false lake, a captive canal. Still waters go nowhere. They encounter edges. Women won't call to them from balconies. No one speaks of flowers . . . or the moon.

And winter comes too soon. Skins bleach. Bones swell up with dampness and the cold. Boats are frozen in a corner of the garden.

They wish for raw confusion. Buildings that press back the sun; bridges that teem with circumstances. Not the knives of the doctors, bleeding winter diseases, the cold eyes of women bored by the court.

Sometimes at night they dream that their bloodstreams have become canals, moving outwards, to the sea. Their lost city, carried here inside the prison of their bodies.

They've forgotten the songs they used to sing.

YOUR HAND CARVES

A city floats
dreaming of Atlantis
I sleep in a bed
carved by your hand

beyond the window
the population whispers
secrets that I harbour
memories I keep

language is the room
I entered to escape you
the journeys taken
the islands abandoned

you have clothed
yourself in vapours
sent letters from
a secret lagoon

I am longing for the amnesia
your hand carves

and then the distance

AN AMUSEMENT IN TWELVE MOVEMENTS

Twelve candles
and a dwarf

Costumes woven
from garden leaves

Giant cogwheels
motivating scenery

Gold slippers

Ribbons, ribbons

He is dressed in a hundred diamonds

Lights from memory: trap doors

A three-cornered hat with bells

Wild boars romp in a sea of flowers

Laughter

A solitary gesture

And my mask
discarded

Artificial Fire

Des jeux de princes qui ne plaisent qu'à ceux qui les font.

– Illustrative quotation from a dictionary

GAMES AND THE KING

Protocol abandoned
he relaxes in the games room
he is fond and warm

and winning every time
a flicker of an eyelid
he gambles much
and loses little

while they listen for
the noise of
their coins in his pocket
he takes the scent of them
into his private rooms

their fingerprints on silver
he takes much of them
in the calm rooms
where the games are

he is fond and warm
winning every time

he leaves little of himself

the scent of them goes farther
they are
paying paying paying
for the favours of a king

WORDS

I've always had too much to say
the witty words   they are shells
from sovereign oceans
an eternal souvenir

pour words in the bodice
wear them
up and down the staircase

threading an amusing necklace
made of words   hear them click
together on the string

I'm spilling them behind my fan
I'm filling up my eyes
with necklace words

later there are silences
emptiness of rooms
he seldom visits

till the string breaks
and words spill like beads

across a marble floor
in search of freer destinations

words

ALL AROUND THE PALACE

You know the women

they have paused in your doorways
run their fingers over
your tapestries

memorized your garden

they have dressed for you
rearranged their features
their faces shine from mirrors

walking through the morning
on their thin ankles
blue veins glowing through
transparent skin
their nerves are humming
out to you

you turn your face away
you know the women

they have paused for
a moment in your doorways
while they are moving
dressed in transparent skins

THE KING ADVISES HIS SON

Never speak to women

unless you speak of flowers
illustrate the garden
and walk with them past fountains

but never let them carry your secrets
they are lapses
barricade the entrance
sing them songs

songs that have heat
put your head on ice
absorb their flesh
ride their passions
wear their fragrance
like a glove

give away nothing
unless it is disposable
fireworks at nightfall
gone from the sky
then gone from the memory
a cut flower
wilting on the stem

walk with them past fountains

don't tell your memories
they will follow
polish their flesh
till it shines
never make a trap of them

never speak to women
walk with them past fountains
fill their eyes with flowers

but never speak to them or
they will come to break you

CHOOSING THE SUBJECT OF THE FOUNTAIN

*The King wanted each of his mistresses represented
allegorically as the subject of a fountain*
                              – Eighteenth-century rumour

The subject that you choose
should cause the fog to gather
somewhere else
should cause the wind to portage
two smooth paths
around its flesh

neither equinoctial storm
nor mechanical thunder
should harm the heart of it
the shine of marble gesture
untouched by pressure
or the dark

glistening streams should
leap from open palms to stroke the
lip and knee and instep
all water should be
rainbowed by the sun
before it penetrates the earth

yet you would choose
pure fountain
as the subject of my fountain
a bright transparent curtain
flung against the trees

something cool and moist
to the touch
a lesser kind of artery

this shower of indefinite diamonds
you can turn it on or off at will

NOTES FOR THE MACHINE AT MARLY

I have a model, gleaming on my table. Cogwheels and cylinders, sharp and smooth. The machine is responsible for fountains. Moving water.

Life in the garden.

I found a larger model in a damp museum, housed in a case of glass and polished wood. Someone had entombed it, given it a brass plaque. I pushed a button and it began to move – even without fountains.

I told a friend in Paris that I like old clockworks. Disconnected from time . . . the predictable click of passing seconds, they become objects free of consequences.   You should see the machine at Marly, he said.

Someone had disconnected it, taken it away. Vanished.

In times of drought a hundred engineers worked the machine at Marly. They bent through the night over tables of rain. They interrupted rivers and creeks, sucked up lakes and ponds. The machine spread its system under the ground. It demanded the Seine, Loire, or Rhone.

A flicker of pleasure grew in the eyes of a king.

In the autumn the north wind and the ghost of a machine at Marly.

How to dismantle such a machine? What to do with its parts?

The garden is stripped of its surfaces. First I remove the fountains, then the statues, remove gravel and grasses and beds of low flowers. I roll up the brown earth. I expose the network of pipes leading to the Machine. Bones of the garden.

Pipes that lead nowhere.

In midsummer the machine becomes tired. I witness the fountains, long for the garden that it never saw, imagine labour. In his daily diary the King remarks that the fountains seem "somewhat reluctant."

The Machine at Marly. Gone.

It pushed and pumped. Everyone admired the fountains. Who admired the machine?

The heartbeat in my dream.

I AM SPEAKING THE DIFFICULT

I am speaking the difficult
syllables of your name
trees block the last day
light   above them
stars scatter

night curves over the end
of the garden I am speaking
grey stone is sliding past
your hip   your shoulder

there is nothing in you that wants
to correct the enunciation
the connection
the difficult syllables
my mispronunciation

I want to tell you
how the river runs
how the garden slides towards it
how stone and earth have spilled
towards the edge

these difficult syllables
are like birds living here
they open their wings and vanish
on any wind that breathes

THE PALACE CLOSED

Yesterday your face shone
out beyond the gates
warm against my palm
its gold became a nugget

today
hard black iron
sharp enough to penetrate the sky
strong enough for denial
and the palace is closed

you mention vague repairs
religious holidays
your shadow travels
through the bars
filters through the windows
passes mirrors turning
darker than your heart

your shadow is locked
your palace is closed

I'm carrying
the glow of your face
here beside the fortune on my hand

vague repairs
religious holidays

patterns in the future
you've imposed upon my life

We were walking in the garden.

Several men with long tapes were measuring two statues – their height, their circumference. We paused to watch their labours.

They finished with one pair of marble figures, and after they had recorded their observations in small grey notebooks, they strolled away from us towards some other sculpture.

We followed. It began to rain. They juggled notebooks, tapes, and umbrellas. Their hands were red from working long hours out of doors. There was a combination of cinder and ink under their nails.

They saw us staring. The statues and the giant urns, they said, had somehow changed location in the last several years. They had been moved a few inches closer or a centimetre or so farther apart. The dimensions of some marbles had expanded while others had shrunk.

My friend pointed out that the palace never seemed to change as long as you stayed in the neighbourhood of the *tapis vert*; that is was always right there, at the top of the stairs, modest and comfortable and precisely the same size. No matter how far, no matter how close. He walked up and down to demonstrate with the palace in full view.

The workmen were uninterested. They turned away, back to their tapes and notebooks. We left them and continued through the rain as far as the Grand Canal.

Later, it seemed that the statues had moved much farther apart but, as my friend said, *the palace stayed there at the top of the stairs*. Unconsciously we paced out the distance between one urn and the next. Passing the place where the men were working we waved to them and their hands fluttered.

We climbed the marble staircase. The hedges on either side opened up like curtains. Staggering, astonishing huge, the palace emerged with wings and floors previously hidden. And still the space . . . continuously remote. The only way to lose that distance was to move around its massive edge and then away, always with our backs turned. Otherwise its image would follow us home.

We walked away. Deep inside the garden a measuring tape revealed the shrinking circumference of a marble thigh.

PLANET

You become the farthest planet

now I can't identify
these marks across your surface
lakes that might be shadows
craters turning dark
towards the sea

and still my notebooks
fill with your reversals
moments from this distance
I can barely understand

I am a prisoner of language
a prisoner of moments
no vehicles have been invented
to bring me any closer

each night the constellations
dance for my approval
the focus of my bent
inverted lens

while I am fixed on you
on moments I can barely understand

I am watching
taking notes

you are a circle of light
ten billion miles away

I am a prisoner of lenses
a prisoner of language

waiting for your bright
deceptive image to respond

TERRE SAUVAGE OR THE KING'S NIGHTMARE

Kings have nightmares. Some dream of revolutionary mobs invading their private chambers . . . torches, knives. My King dreams of Terre Sauvage.

The Royal Gardener pauses. He unrolls a map of New France. Thin pencil lines reveal a garden plan. This pleases the King. He doffs his hat, mutters a few suggestions.

Miraculously, ships filled with hundreds of workmen arrive. The task of removing the giant primal forest begins. The first layer, undergrowth and bush, is removed. To the King's horror another layer of bush appears in seconds. Thicker than the first. No axe can penetrate its growth.

Winter arrives, halting the project for ten months.

The following year Le Notre suggests they double the number of workmen and import trained French executioners to fell the trees. This pleases the King. He doffs his hat, re-examines the plan. He objects to the shapes of the decorative waters. They look like nothing more than a chain of great big lakes emptying into a canal, thin and irregular. Meaningless.

Le Notre explains that they will make fine ice rinks for winter sports.

The executioners have finally downed the trees. They begin sketching out allées and parterres upon the exposed earth. They begin digging and locate solid rock ten inches down.

Everything suddenly appears to change. The King finds himself alone, in a thick forest, his distance perception, sense of direction, completely addled. Light barely passes through the trees.

Somewhere, vaguely to his left, there is a loud roaring noise, like wind. He stumbles through thorns and burs in the direction of thunder. Bits of Royal brocade are left on branches.

He comes upon the waterfall. He is completely stunned. It lacks symmetry but none the less it is vaster than any waterwork he has ever seen. He wonders how Le Notre was able to design anything so powerful. He doffs his cerebral hat and imagines how greatly this will impress other monarchs. He decides to present Le Notre with a dukedom.

And then his foot slips on wet rocks. He plunges sceptre, robe and mantle into the churning rapids and flies over. He feels he has become the very centre of a fountain. SCREAMING.

The following week he eliminates the word *glory* from his vocabulary.

NECESSARY PAUSE

A necessary pause
precedes the performance
just before dawn
splits open to morning

the hard morning pauses
they have held your shirt
caressed your stockings

pauses
moments turn back
those eyes that sweep
the crowd

they carry your relics
contemplate fountains

footsteps leave no traces
and the handwriting is burned

BIRDS

He cannot make them stay
or stay out of the garden
they make their own decisions

he considers cages
giant aviaries
a mesh of metal among
the trees he has planted

some stay
others perch on the outside wire
they sing louder
disturb his morning sleep

the dogs of the hunt
whimper

some birds migrate farther south
they leave him looking for
their patterns in the sky

he desires the tiny hearts
of birds as jewellery
he invents special weapons to interrupt
their flight

generations later
their fragile eggs break
expose a path of grace notes
unharnessed by his will
it connects the garden

He chooses this location because there is no view.

> Here he can keep his personality intact. His lust tied.
> Directly in front of the palace there is a large hill. The small immediate garden is enclosed on either side by steep cliffs. There is little he can do. This is comforting, at least at first.
> He cannot live there. But he will visit, and bring along his favourites. He believes he will flourish in the company of temporary intimacy and accessible green.

> He can't sleep. The cliffs cancel his dreams. There is a pressure on the left and right sides of his brain. He is convinced that the hill has moved closer. Twelve different engineers measure the distance from his bed to the first incline of earth. They assure him nothing has changed. He realizes this is the problem.

> He levels the hill.

> During his morning promenade the attending crowd is thin, the atmosphere informal. They chat and giggle in his presence. No one discusses glory or divine right, and the girls turn their eyes to younger men.

> He cuts into cliffs, expands the castle. There is an army draining the enormous outlying swamp. Soldiers in their hundreds die of diseases connected to unhealthy soil. The engineers bring water to the fountains at his palaces.

He builds four hundred fountains down through the vista where the hill used to be.

He dismantles, builds four hundred more.

Two thousand oak trees are brought in from the forests of the Jura. Half die in the process of transplantation. They are replaced with healthy giants. Well-ordered forests appear where once the cliffs used to be. But now they present a barrier to his view from the west and east rooms of the palace. A throbbing begins in his temples. The forests disappear. The are replaced by artificial lakes. Hundreds of guests float in imported gondolas.

He demands and receives a large cascade where each of his mistresses is represented in stone as either a goddess or a water nymph. More forests appear where once there was only mud and toads. These he sees from his bedrooms, though they are five miles away!

He has broken the intimacy of rock and swamp wide open.

Now he feels much better.

Sleep.

TURNING BACK AT DUSK

These are deceptive spaces

windows bronze
a cold stone warms

I'm trying to connect
the break in the horizon
moving distance after distance

there are canals
thin as gold leaf
and dreams of fountains
collapsing at the edge

trees that tremble
just beyond my hand
are miles and miles away
the oval mirror of the lake
impossible to reach

I am trying to move
distance after distance

turning back at dusk
my declaration of withdrawal

I see the garden
as near to me
and as far away

The Poisoned Shirt

A third chamber, as it were the anteroom of the above, is correctly named the decaying chamber ... the walls are enormously thick.

– Saint-Simon

SOME OTHER GARDEN

The doctors come blindfolded
into the palace

they deliver babies
borne by masked women

anonymous screaming flesh

children
pulled from the womb
torn from the arms

the anonymous
flesh of the palace
taken to grow in
some other garden

next evening
the women perform at the ball
prepare their cards for the table

tiny fists
close up in their brains

THE PORCELAIN TRIANON

The only thing I ever asked
was porcelain
a playhouse here
among the trees

you gave me faience
pretending to be porcelain

see the pools outside the door
blue and white
blue and white
convince me that is porcelain

porcelain and privacy
you gave me a forest of spyglasses
focusing on faience

blue and white
convince me this is porcelain

and permanence
unfolding here without
your strict approval
I want to keep
my small false castle
built within the time
frame of a miracle

the tiny garden with its urns
blue and white

you tear it down
because you cannot change it
improve it or expand it

the little structure
worked upon a lie

blue and white
blue and white
imaginary porcelain

shards sing
all around your feet

THE ANONYMOUS JOURNAL

Today I walked as far as the Trianons – an incredible distance. The garden around moves from one point to another. You do not pass it by like any other landscape. It crawls by you and the weather changes before it moves.

I walk away from the palace in a light drizzle, arriving at the Trianons with the sun full in the sky. It is broken into splinters on the west arm of the canal.

I arrive, realizing that there is very little of him left there. All that remains is one intimate allée, designed by Le Notre for a porcelain playhouse.

The whole geography has moved smoothly into another time.

And there is not a sign of me. The Trianon de Porcelaine is broken. I remain in a neutral room on the north side of the palace, fading into crowds of courtiers.

Walking back towards the palace I have to face the wind. It is almost dark.

EVIDENCE

There were traces
there was evidence

the room moved in to
hold it
like a dark gold frame

we staggered round like saints
tiny ships sailed at our heels
lilies came to light

all evidence
the letter on the table
the ashes in the grate

until the day the dove
emerged

silent from your mouth

LE ROI S'AMUSE

The man who touches you
without love
arrives in a golden coach
drawn by a purebred horse

he carries his hands to you
like old sorrows

he is the death
of the child in you
the beginning of dark
there are no more songs
from the rooms
he moves through

the mouth he puts to yours
contains a brutal statement
your limbs become machinery
to the limits he enforces

he doesn't lure you into
altered landscapes
keeps his time in
artificial daylight
speaking solid words

and the last glimpse of
his sail on the horizon
never finishes

the stones that felt his step
the sea   the bed that you return to
all remember him

his breath remains
forever at your throat

remember him

THE VERMILION BOX

Poison comes in phials filled with liquids, or packets filled with powders. It can be eaten, drunk, injected, or absorbed through the skin. Choose the scent. Often it is disguised as perfume.

Madame de Montespan, not yet old, but fat from too many babies, registers extreme disapproval. The King is slinking secretly off to other beds. She wants to perfume the Venetian lace at his throat. She wants to powder his wig.

No more aphrodisiacs. She administers them. He moves like a magnet to the iron charms of Madame de Fontagnes. She wants to sweeten that lady's tea, colour her eau de cologne.

Arsenic, opium, antimony, hemlock. Sitting alone in her rooms she shakes her head slightly. *Red sulphur, bat's blood dried dust of moles, yellow sulphur.*

Poison, a ritual extending from her body. The chalice rests on her stomach, her breasts fall away from her ribcage. It is the older woman, more wrinkled than herself. She whispers incantations and recipes into her ears. The younger one offers her flesh, like ripe fruit for the appetite of some darker power.

Iron filings, resin of dried plums.

She is falling, falling from favour. She hates him. She loves him. She sees him dead, surrounded by satin then safe in the tomb. *Her* poison trapped in his body like sperm in a uterus.

During the ceremony she spells his name backwards on her inner thigh in donkey's blood. She spells his name forwards with some of her own. Someone saves the knife for a Baroque Forensic lab.

Decades later she pays four young women to remain in her room from nightfall to dawn. At her request they play cards and drink wine for ten dark hours. They laugh, gossip, while she hides behind the velvet curtains remembering the poison that perfumed her dreams.

She thinks of the still, warm, dead heart of a pigeon, housed in a vermilion box, said to have power, but useless without the bird itself, without flight. Finally it had bloated, become putrid, had to be disposed of along with the box that held it.

Beyond the curtains the women discuss their lovers in the warm glow of the candles. Their smooth hands finger the cards nervously.

Madame de Montespan closes the lid on the poison.

HORSES

In fields that unfurl to
the left of the garden
twelve grey horses
ease into canter

their loins adjust to
the three-beat rhythm

breaking like thunder
deep in the forest
flashing by branches
trampling moss

I never see them
here in this dream where
I'm pacing my limbs to
the nod of the trainer

here in this dream
educated muscle
covers the length of
my bones

I remember
clouds of rhythm
surrounding the palace

his step on the stair
his key in the lock

the supple behaviour

the hunt and the harness
unyielding

THE YEARS DEPARTING

Coaches departing
are the years pulling away
stern   their private latches
closed on cool compartments

once I wept the distance
remembering the pressure
limb on limb
and the landscape outside
ringing like time

you coasting from my view

from balconies I have seen
you coast from my view
I have seen you hunched
like a thief over the wheel
of the months turning

another year towards closure

the inevitable closure

quiet click
of the door's latch
how I bolt it afterwards
the metal hard against my hand

THE POISONED SHIRT

The poison is absorbed
into the meat of his back
the muscle

I want it to travel
nerves   sinews
chords of tissue
to answer the pluck of pain

I want to kill from without

the whole man
his body absorbing the entire
corruption

a final message from
blood to brain
until it bubbles away

the last sentence
frozen in his eyes

and me answering

Glass Coffins

It was not wise to leave so precious a relic in an undefended place outside the walls of town . . . because in those days a saint's body was esteemed more than a treasure.

– The Little Flowers of Saint Clare

ANONYMOUS JOURNAL

During this long winter we rarely go outside, though it is seldom warmer in our rooms. The interior of the palace has become a condensed winter world – cold mirrors, frozen chandeliers. Our fogged breath precedes us everywhere, softening candelabra and fresco.

It is as if the garden has completely disappeared. We can hear the wind and the groaning of the giant trees. But we never see outside. Thousands of window panes are covered by a thick frost.

There are no more gold settings at the table. Too much warmth in the cutlery is ridiculous. Soon the silver will disappear as well, reducing us to crockery.

It is February and we are surprised by a miraculous sun. He insists that we move outdoors, walk in his white garden. We don't object, put on our cloaks and boots, leave rooms for the first time in months.

At first we are overcome by endless snow and the shock of the first cold swallow of air, fresh on the tissues of our lungs. But when we can see again we are amazed by the unbroken surface of white and the open blue of the sky. The ground plan of the garden is erased by winter.

The statues are confused, awkward under hats and epaulets of snow. Urns grow ice. Our steps are new marks, making new boundaries.

We move towards the Bassin D'Apollon, watching as the metal forms take shape against white. We are able to pick out the four horses, the sea monster, the torso of the young god emerging from his chariot. The wind has swept all the snow away from the Bassin, revealing enclosed ice, thick as marble. The sculpture is now locked, changed completely, made impotent by ice.

He, standing there looking at this, understands for the first time that all his monuments are immovable, frozen in their own time. They are like novelties on display, already under glass.

The Sun God and his Chariot, powerless in a cold, cold season.

The light, the wind, revealing all of this. Making the image totally clear. And totally brutal.

WINTER OF 1709

You rearrange the lace
at your wrist with cold fingers
the freeze deepens

hens are laying frozen eggs
behind the kitchen garden
blossoms are trapped in the false
promise of tubers

cold days
the last time
I wore this cloak against
the weather I noticed

how velvet remains unaffected
by the breeze   fades only
when the sun touches it
over and over

the sun no longer reaches me
the colour of this cold
is permanent
when trees become cathedral
bones over our heads

you add another acre
to the dormant garden
ice silvers steps and paths
and fountains

your finger prints
on everything you touch

SILENCED

Autumn
false gold falling on actuality
stone walls all around

summer hid the prison
the perfect palace
draped in green and growing
overtop the stairs

winter now
and every word is opened
syllables ride to the horizon
in the grim hands of the post

false gold covers gravel
nothing hides in green

this palace
this prison

built in time
to silence
every loss I speak

LADY REASON

Emotionally
I am not yet ready for
Madame de Maintenon

Your Solidity
he calls her   or
Lady Reason

she answering
Majesty
Majesty

he bows
to the superior religion
she holds up a mirror to
his crime

his passion
the vanity of wars
and women won

landscapes pillaged

Lady Reason
Lady Reason
you move in a different realm

pulling out the power of
the lust of a King

his will to control
the world
himself

I am not ready for you

I am still
running through crooked
paths in my imagination

ONE MEMORY OF OPENING

With nothing to hold
I remember open windows
a garden or lake beyond
you holding me

how our clothing opened
and closed again   like windows
the night or light entering
us pouring out

surely there is more than this
one memory of opening
the breeze from the world
around us   a sail on the lake
crowds waiting on the shore

wind on my sleeve
a sail suddenly pregnant
the ease with which
we fell together then
and fell apart

DOCTOR FAGON

We reason with one another, he prescribes the remedies, I omit to take them and I recover. *Molière*

Doctor Fagon killed them all. I saw his window the other day, filled with blades. Enormous scissors intersecting the rectangle. *And knives, knives.*

Doctor Fagon enters the chamber in a brown cloak. He bleeds the Queen. Laundresses delight in sheets stained royally red.

Doctor Fagon performs his operations by the light of a thousand candles. Muscles, soft to the scalpel, open over royal bone. The silversmiths are busy building reliquaries all across the country.

Earthworms against gout.
Bees' ashes to make hair grow.
Ant oil against deafness.

Doctor Fagon senses hidden smallpox deep in the palace. He administers emetics. Three princes vomit their way to heaven. The iron heart of a King breaks open in the carriage on the way to Marly.

Doctor Fagon mixes powders long into the night. He rebukes those that avoid him, accuses them of impiety. Museums prepare for his mortar and pestle.

He prepares for the King.

Doctor Fagon broods over Burgundy wine. He doses the King with spirit of amber, rubs his left leg with hot cloths, wraps the royal limbs in linen soaked in brandy.

Eventually the pain evaporates. It leaves the palace by the back door, hovers somewhere east of the Grand Canal.

Doctor Fagon cures the King. *The King is dead.*

GLASS COFFINS

The women longed for glass coffins. They imagined that centuries later men would file by to wonder at their incorrupt flesh. They were also interested in satin pillows and narrow couches. I know that is true. One told me so herself.

Glass coffins. Like the one the friars built around the body of Saint Clare. Like the one that dwarfs placed Snow White in. And these women *had* been kissed and kissed by their prince.

Often the women chose their costumes for the sake of glass coffins. They knew their fabric held together longest.

They arranged their hair in deathless styles.

Between the covers, under the glass, their bodies shine.

HALL OF MIRRORS

Overhead the crystal hangs
handfuls of tears
in placid air

the mirrors divide
my body darkens
waiting in the hall

see me in the glass
reflected
see me in the glass
abandoned

I am walking back and forth
in a dream
never changing
my costume or my mind

I am blind
from staring too long at the sun

the scent of a King
is still in my hair

II.

ELEVEN POEMS FOR LE NOTRE

In the gardens the King never says outright "Do not accompany me." When you meet him he halts and if he bows after saying a few words you must walk on. If he wishes you to stay, he asks you to walk with him. Otherwise you simply can't.

– Duchesse D'Orleans

Princes were in the moral world what monsters were in the physical; we saw openly in them the vices that are unseen in other men.

– Duchesse Du Maine

I

I was walking in the garden of his imaginary palace
he had chosen silence and indefinite vacations
there was nothing to clean up afterwards

except the season
which shed its possibilities all along the pathways
and the horizon
which carried sails of ships I had not visited
as I was walking

            in the garden of his imaginary
palace planting episodes and confrontations
bits of history for fine dust
and despite the promise of my delicate rehearsals
despite the maps that he'd proved true to scale
all that lay beneath the surface of the soil
I'd come to alter
was a river of thickened ink

and it appeared that over and over
I had a black thumb

II

His position
                mine
a crazy axiom of linear perspective
the function of that garden

                              painters stoop to it
as if the world were solid   architectural
but colour softens up their distances
green emptying to blue

                              no colour there
we walked   kept to the walls when possible
expecting that predictable geometry would save us
in the end from paths of intersection

and then events became confused degrees of angles
something we intended did not flex
broke through the surfaces of diagrams and entered
structure

        so that even now
two hundred well placed orange trees lead off
to nowhere   bulbs pulsing underground anticipate
survival

      we're stopped here   frozen
to the marble of the balustrade

where vanishing points
beckon

III

Before I came to move again
this man prepared to organize
restrain the landscape
                         a simple act
of laying hold of paper pencil ruler
a protractor

and clumsy shovels
projecting from the end of several brown arms
no complex survey tools   the paths he chose were
marked by hand with chalk
or maybe twisted ribbon

back to design   the arrows on the paper which follow
to the target of translation
they projected from the eye and then the arm
of what would seem a softer individual but
long before the workmen bent to turn aside
the first inch of the earth
    design had settled
hard in this man's head

more like concrete
than a garden

IV

Thresholds existed
and I might have voyaged out at any moment
past the rusted cage of gates
                                      and into
intense disorder

instead I walked for months around
ambitious cultivation   aware of intervals of timber
and of fountains   the scrape of rake against
a thousand pebbles
the dull insistent questions of the statues

and when his smile exposed the iron teeth
of garden tools
I felt the silver of the thresholds glisten
out to me

but I was captured by his will   the formal garden
and welded too by indecision
to the holy taste of ash
around his mouth

v

In winter trees exploded up against the sky
like black fireworks
                they touched
to make the tunnels that I moved through

the sun is gone I thought until I captured its reflection
in the dirty water of canals
                        and then I took it
in my eyes and held it there
the after image burning permanent diamonds
on the folds inside my brain

these were the personal adornments
that I carried with me always
always
so I could not see around them or beyond them
could not see beyond them

                        out to the shadow
of another burning image
                he
walking unescorted through the garden
half a mile away

VI

Dust on satin
the soft hems of my clothing

and I believed it pleasant to carry something
of the garden to my wardrobe
        like silver powder drawn
to me by some remote
magician
   pleasanter let's say
than stunted vegetation

reality made dirt of it of course
and quickly cleaned it from the tissue of my skirts
the brass and bristle of the clothes brush
in the cool hands of the servants
their motions so deliberate
      and so angry

it was the way they disapproved of me that brushed aside
the traces of peculiar recreations
the way they disapproved of subtle dust
on satin
   and all those mornings that I emptied
free of time

    walking walking walking
    in that foolish garden

VII

Spring was worst

a little wind would settle in
warm moist disorganized
pushing line away from the clutch of centre
tossing back the gathered skirts
of unchecked form
and overlooking the importance of security
and then ignoring the obvious yellow
of old well draughted plans

his plans

serenely twisted in the ugly shape
of pollarded trees or frozen
in the ridiculous gestures of the statues
until a little wind nudged ice aside and introduced
a growth to other
than his plans

        that was the season he
attacked the garden like a furious disease
working it with weapons from his wheelbarrow
cutting back
cutting back until like every other thing
he ever showed me

                        spring
and that glorious garden
                           were entirely
in his power

VIII

Frost all over the garden softening green to grey
scale   the day he returned there was frost all

over the garden and an onion skin of ice on the
discontinued fountains

he returned   riding his horse with the glass eyes
riding him
needing no blinkers to camouflage his blindnesses

and all that white frost cancelling colour once again
except for

>   the black of his thoughtless re entry
>   and the blue of our cold celebrations

IX

On summer evenings they roll out from a man's feet
until the fading out of light

                          glued
to the flatness of the ground
like rich shaped beds of earth
they glide past the mockery of monuments
and approach his architectural repertoire

where
    finding walls
they bend in improbable locations
mid thigh or straight across the rib cage
forming new pliable joints for his confident
anatomy

        the shadow illustrates the man
submissive   curving when he least expects
to the fact of his own authority

long cast shadows
draughting out the spirit of the man
to the fawning shape of a bow
and he is broken

                in the custody
of his own enforced obedience

X

Someone down the hall was working on his monument
I was riding like a sunset on the edge
of altered landscape
this proves I never was his widow

the rasping cough of chisel on the marble
created thirty feathers for the left wing of an angel
the jewellery he gave me was sliding to my knuckles
well cut stones of hot intended blood

technicians for his tomb arrived in numbers
to offer praise and redesign
his life for him their manners were dramatic
and assured   the same as all his other false
invented memories

I was riding to the fire of the sun
it balanced on a side aisle of the garden
and I never really was
                              and am not now
his widow

though all these fishless ponds can reproduce for me
the darker shade of colour in my clothing

XI

I am walking in the garden of his imaginary palace
I do not need a guidebook anymore
I am completely familiar with the laws of puzzle
inflicted by his gravel pathways   I am completely

familiar with the unexpected statues that interrupt
his forest   and like the moths that every night
invade the lamps along the terrace
I'm moved towards a fire under glass

                                            this landscape
so controlled as to deflect my need to burn
or to extinguish   to bring about a quick decided
finish   I am walking in the garden of his imaginary
palace   where I feel the icy glass against my cheek

and while I fumble in my pockets for a purpose
all his green cathedrals turn to brown
his fountains to reflecting pools

                                            crows clutter up
the sky and gates of autumn still grind soft to close

and then in time to cage
the winter

Photo Credits for *Some Other Garden*

Photographs of Versailles by Jennifer Dickson, R.A.

p. i: "Near the Grand Trianon." Allée leading from the Grand Trianon, to infinity.

p. 1: "Sphinx: the Belvedere." Near the Petit Trianon, Versailles.

p. 3: "The French Pavilion." Near the Petit Trianon, Versailles.

p. 17: "Through the Crystal Wall." Reflections of Mique's Belvedere; northwest gardens of the Petit Trianon, Versailles.

p. 43: "Late afternoon: the Grand Trianon." The Garden Drawing Room of the Grand Trianon, Versailles.

p. 59: "Archway through the Queen's cabbagepatch." Hameau de la Reine, Versailles.

p. 73: "Dawn Nymph." Fontaine du point du jour, Versailles.